Published in 2022 by Orange Mosquito

An Imprint of Welbeck Children's Limited
part of Welbeck Publishing Group.

Based in London and Sydney.

www.welbeckpublishing.com

Design and layout © Mosquito Books Barcelona, SL 2021
Text © Mia Cassany 2021
Illustration © Iker Ayestaran 2021
Translated by Howard Curtis
Publisher: Margaux Durigon
Production: Clare Hennessy

ISBN: 9781914519185
eISBN: 9781914519192
Printed in China

10 9 8 7 6 5 4 3 2 1

FSC
www.fsc.org
MIX
Paper from
responsible sources
FSC® C020056

No animals were harmed in the making of this book, but a few were bribed into helping out.

SPORTS HEROES

Inspiring tales of athletes who stood up and stood out

Mia Cassany · Iker Ayestaran

ORANGE
M·O·S·Q·U·I·T·O

Muhammad Ali

Louisville, Kentucky (USA), 1942
Scottsdale, Arizona, (USA), 2016

Muhammad Ali (his name was Cassius Clay, but he changed it) was born into a poor artistic family in Louisville. His father was a painter who did what he could to make a living. Ali was a brave, restless boy who was angered at the racial injustice he suffered every day. He would come home upset and covered in bruises; he was always getting into trouble at school,

rebelling against the prejudices that existed between people based on the color of their skin. One day, on the way home, his bicycle was stolen and it was then that he met a policeman named Joe E. Martin, who gave him the best advice of his life: "All the anger and resentment you feel about injustice, let it out on a punch bag, before you go hitting anybody."

Martin started training Ali and realized that he was dealing with a true champion. Ali was soon competing and before long his shelves were filled with medals and trophies. In 1964 he became heavyweight boxing champion of the world. But the charisma and the rebelliousness Ali had had since he was a child were still there and drove him to speak up publicly against racial segregation and war. He continued rebelling against everything, and in the end the government took away his titles and gave him a prison sentence which was overturned by the Supreme Court. But none of this mattered to Ali. He continued fighting injustice and later in life was celebrated for the important role he played in bringing attention to the issue of racism.

Dick Fosbury

Portland, Oregon (USA), 1947

It is rare to encounter innovation in the world of sport. The rules are very strict, and the techniques that sportspeople use to achieve success are usually the same. But what happens if you make it to an Olympic high jump competition knowing that your chances of winning are very low?

That is what happened to Fosbury in the Olympic Games in Mexico in 1968. He measured over 6.3 feet, and being so tall he could not master the high jump using the traditional straddle technique, however hard he tried and however much he trained. Far from being discouraged or accepting defeat, Fosbury changed the style of his jump, developing one in which he curved his back and bent his legs over the bar.

On the first day of the competition everyone looked at Fosbury in surprise, thinking he had gone mad. "Nobody jumps like that," said the fans in amazement. But gradually they realized that Fosbury was achieving the best jumps of everyone competing. He soon won the gold medal and broke the Olympic record.

He was unable to take part in the next Olympics but, to the surprise of many, 28 of the 40 jumpers used his technique, which was named the Fosbury Flop. Even today, jumpers use it. Fosbury demonstrated that if something is not tailor-made for you, you can adapt and create something better.

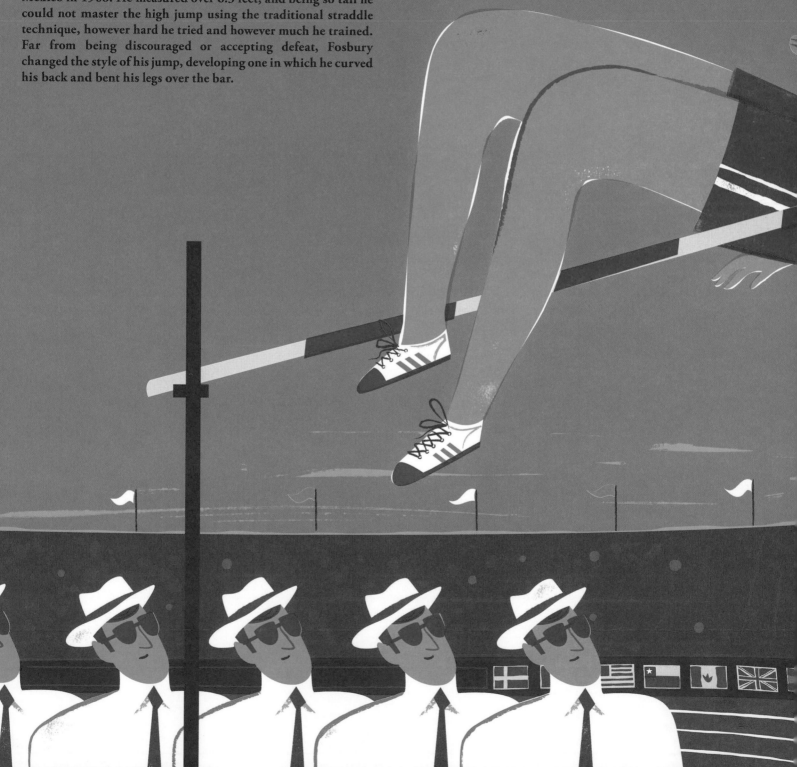

Gerry Lopez

Honolulu, Hawaii (USA), 1948

It could be said that Gerry Lopez was born with a surfboard under his arm. At the age of seven, Lopez started surfing major waves and before long became one of the youngest surfers to master the incredible and very complicated waves of Pipeline, a spot in Hawaii. Pipeline became world famous in the 1970s; the bravest and most daring surfers traveled there from all over the world to try and surf the biggest waves ever seen.

Lopez soon realized that it was easy for him to dominate the waves with the long surfboards that were popular at the time, but he was an inquisitive young man with a great desire to learn and he thought that he could do better.

Lopez created some short boards which were much more complicated to use but also more flexible. With these new boards, his movements were short and intense, and Lopez was able to move over the waves more easily. This dance between the surfer and the waves was so beautiful that many others started to follow in his footsteps, unwittingly creating surfing as we know it today.

As Gerry Lopez himself says: "Life, like waves, is changeable, and you have to learn to dance to its sound or it will pass you by. You have to be spontaneous and always want more and try to go further."

Edurne Pasaban

Tolosa, Gipuzkoa (Spain), 1972

In 2010, Edurne Pasaban became the first woman to climb all 14 eight-thousanders: the highest mountains on Earth, located in the Himalayas. This is the hardest challenge for any mountaineer and it took Pasaban almost ten years of determination and improvement to achieve this feat.

Pasaban's first expedition to the Himalayas was in 1998, when she tried to climb her first eight-thousander. This attempt ended only 892 feet (272 meters) from the peak due to the impassable amount of accumulated snow. She didn't reach the top until 9 years later. The same thing happened on Everest. It took Pasaban three attempts to reach the summit when she became the third Spanish woman to do it.

On her seventh eight-thousander, Pasaban suffered severe frostbite during the descent and was unable able to finish. This threw her into a deep depression, and for the first time in her life, Pasaban was on the verge of giving up, forgetting about climbing, and leaving the mountains behind forever. But her courage and her desire to improve won out after a year, and she returned with more strength than ever having learned the most important lesson in life: getting to the summit means not only completing a difficult journey, but also realizing that in order to win, we have to accept that sometimes we will lose.

Gertrude Ederle

New York (USA), 1905 – Wyckoff (USA), 2003

Gertrude Ederle's passion grew out of her greatest fear: at a young age she fell into a lake and, being unable to swim, thought she would drown. From that moment on, Ederle decided she would learn to swim and to enjoy being in the water. Then, while still young, Ederle caught measles which left her with poor hearing. The doctors advised her to give up swimming, but it was too late; Ederle had fallen in love with it and kept on going until she achieved major successes. At the age of 15, Ederle took part in the Olympic Games in Paris, winning the gold medal in the 400 meter freestyle relay and two bronze medals. When she was only 19, she became the first woman to swim the English Channel and she carried on to complete a number of long sea crossings.

The press began calling her Miss Gertrude Ederle, Queen of the Waves.

Ederle swam and swam and continued to improve, but her hearing problems returned, more serious each time. She would try to ignore them, but finally Ederle was forced to retire from competition. Once more, as she had when she had fallen into that lake as a child, she decided that she would fight against what scared her. She was determined not to let everything she had learned go to waste: she began to coach children in a school for the deaf in New York, teaching them not only to move their arms in water but to swim despite their difficulties.

Jackie Robinson

Cairo, Georgia (USA), 1919
Stamford, Connecticut (USA), 1972

Although Jackie Robinson is without any doubt one of the greatest sportspeople and best-known figures in the world of baseball, what really made him a legend was his activities in the civil rights movement of the 1960s.

Robinson was a master baseball player and even when he was very young all the talent scouts saw his potential. No team could afford to turn him down, and he finally became the first black American player able to take part in Major League Baseball.

During his first games, Robinson suffered all kinds of taunts and insults from his own team's fans, who could not accept a black player – they even threw black cats at him to bring him bad luck. But he ignored them. He kept playing, improving every day, demonstrating that the aggression of racists could not destroy him or his dream of being a professional baseball player.

Robinson's determination and courage won him the respect of fellow players. During one of his games – there were many journalists present, but only the insults of the spectators could be heard – his teammate Pee Wee Reese went up to him, embraced him, and cried: "You can hate a man for many reasons. Color is not one of them."

On April 15, 1947, Robinson made his debut with the Dodgers; 50 years later, every team in Major League Baseball (MLB) decided to retire his uniform number, 42, as a symbol that baseball is not only for white people. In addition, every April 15 since then this historic change is remembered, and all the players wear the number 42.

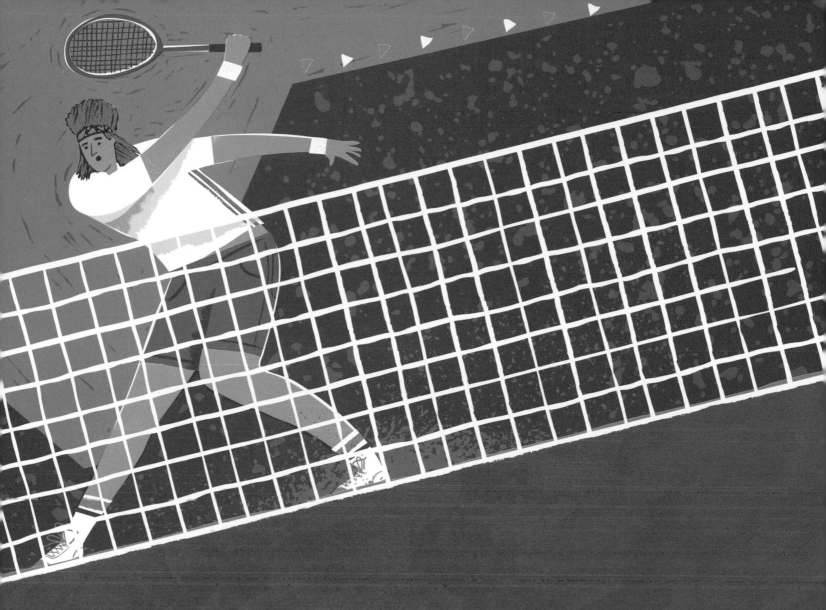

Andre Agassi

Las Vegas, Nevada (USA), 1970

Andre Agassi didn't like tennis and never would have chosen to play the sport, let alone take it up professionally, but it turned out that tennis liked Andre Agassi.

Agassi's father made up his mind to turn his son into a famous tennis player, whatever it cost. Agassi paid very dearly for this decision: he was forced to train all hours of the day and sometimes even at night, with no time for playing with friends or enjoying himself. He soon learned that the only way to keep his father happy was to win games and Agassi won one game after another with an intense and angry playing style. The public admired Agassi more and more, while also envying his outwardly successful life.

With each strike, Agassi learned that winning was everything and the image we project matters, even if it has nothing to do with how we feel inside.

Agassi started to rebel against expectations by playing important championships in jeans, or wearing a flashy blond wig to hide the fact that he was losing his hair.

Over time, Agassi calmed down with the realization that it is all right to show our weaknesses: it's the one thing that makes us stronger.

Sonja Henie

Oslo (Norway), 1912 – 1969

Sonja Henie was a great lover of sport and competition from a very young age. Athletics came completely naturally to her. She was exposed to it at home: her father was a well-known world cycling champion and her mother loved dancing, so how could she be any other way?

Henie settled on ice-skating as her sport – and quickly rose to the top. At the age of 11, Henie began to win titles and achieved her first Olympic gold at 15. She won the Olympics three times in total and was a world champion ten times! Henie was unstoppable.

Henie's specialty was figure skating, a difficult and traditionally very methodical form of skating – with her sensitivity and courage, succeeded in changing it forever.

Before Henie, female skaters were definite in their movements, strict to follow technique; Henie changed all of this when she introduced the fluid movements of dancing to her skating style. One day, to everyone's surprise, she arrived for a competition in a short skirt. It was the first time this had happened in the history of skating! But there was no doubt this garment allowed greater flexibility of movement.

As always happens when people are confronted with something new, some criticized Henie – but she changed the landscape of figure skating forever. Now, wonderful dance routines are ubiquitous, as are short skirts which help the judges score skaters' movements! Henie's true victory was her fearlessness to change the rules of the game in order to create an even more beautiful sport.

Pelé

Minas Gerais (Brazil), 1940

Edson Arantes do Nascimento, known throughout the world as Pelé, was born in one of the poorest places in Brazil. He was surrounded by a loving family, sharing his father's passion for soccer.

In 1950 Brazil lost to Uruguay in the World Cup Final. This moment defined Pelé. He saw his father, usually a very cheerful man, weeping and very upset about the defeat. There and then, in front of everyone, he promised that he would win the championship and dedicate it to his father.

Nobody believed that this boy, who had no money and nothing in his favor, would be an example of determination and that he would make an almost impossible dream come true. Pelé trained hard, but it was his fighting spirit that ensured he would never give up his goal and this led him to win the World Cup, just as he had promised his father. Pelé won the Cup not just once, but 3 times –no other player in the world has won it this many times.

Many years later, when Pelé had become a world-famous soccer legend, his mother gave him the old shoeshine kit he had used as a boy; in it was a coin, the first money he earned. His mother had kept it there all those years. It was a beautiful way of reminding her son where he had come from and how far he had gone, and all thanks to determination. A dream come true!

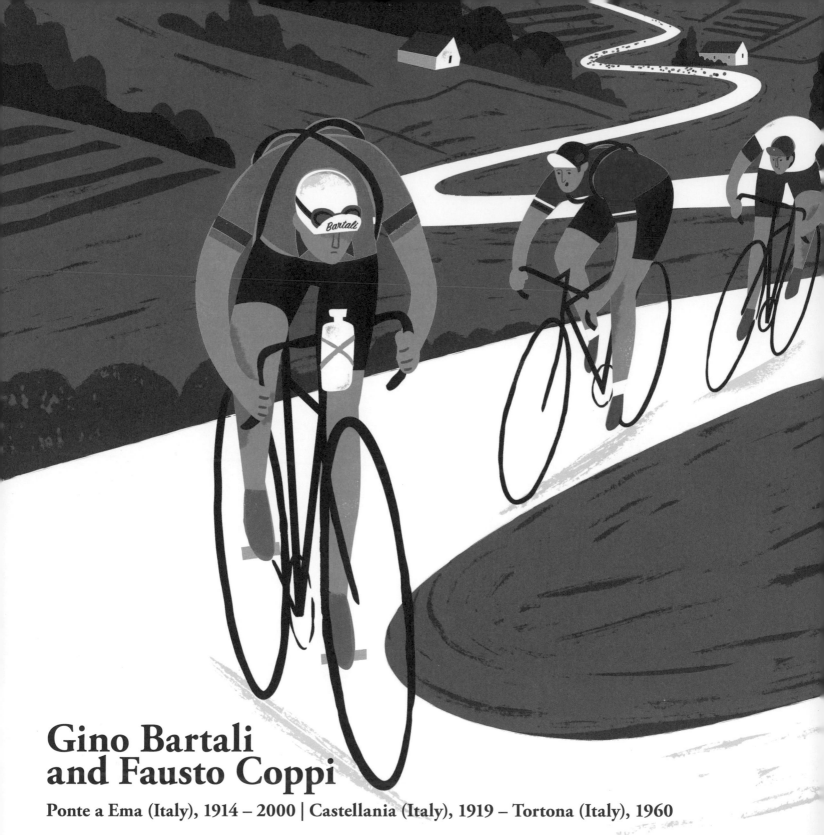

Gino Bartali and Fausto Coppi

Ponte a Ema (Italy), 1914 – 2000 | Castellania (Italy), 1919 – Tortona (Italy), 1960

It is said that true competition only exists where there is strong rivalry: something demonstrated by these two Italian cyclists throughout their careers.

Bartali and Coppi were the best cyclists of their generation. Every year they competed for the Giro d'Italia, the Tour de France, and other important trophies: they rode side by side – competing in each other's shadow.

What's more, as if they were characters in a film, they were polar opposites. Bartali was conservative and reliable, clear in his intentions and strategies; a traditional, elegant Italian, well-mannered and impeccably stylish. Coppi, on the other hand, was a moody and unpredictable introvert, his performances depended on the inspiration of the moment, but he was revolutionary in his ideas. They were the perfect combination, and the public loved both of them.

Coppi won the Giro d'Italia five times and the Tour de France twice. Bartali won the Giro d'Italia three times and also won the Tour de France twice. It was not until after his death, though, that Bartali's greatest achievement came to light. During the Second World War, Bartali had carried false passports hidden inside his bicycle, helping more than 800 Jews escape to safety! Although nobody knows this for certain, many people believe that Bartali only shared this secret with his greatest rival, who never revealed it.

SWISS TIMING

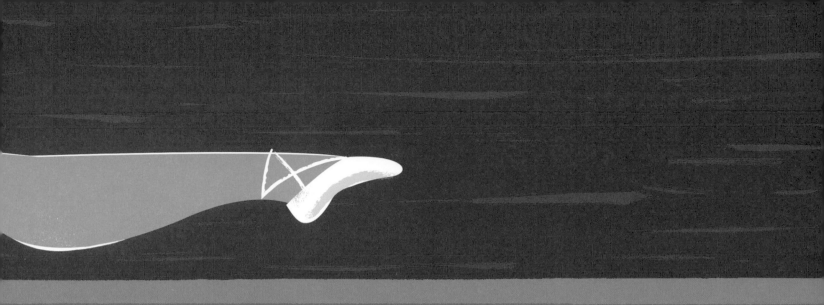

Nadia Comăneci

Onesti (Romania), 1961

Before Nadia Comăneci, it was believed by Olympic judges that no sports person could ever achieve perfection – a score of 10 – in a gymnastic routine. As far as they were concerned, there was no such thing as perfection; there were always little things that could be improved. The judges were very tough in their assessments and were convinced that nobody would ever make them change their minds. But then a very young Comăneci got up on the bars and performed the most perfect routine the judges had seen in their lives. Comăneci received the first 10 in the history of the Olympic Games – and it would not be her last!

It was quite an amusing moment – the scoreboards were only programmed to show three digits and couldn't show a 10. Comăneci's score had to be shown as 1.00, and the Dutch judge in charge of the scoring had to wave his arms and shout from the table: "It's a 10, it's a 10, not a 1!"

Fortunately, these days scoreboards are prepared for perfection.

Katherine Switzer

Amberg (Germany), 1947

Katherine Switzer was the first woman to take part in a marathon with a registered entry number. Until 1967 the Boston Marathon had been a sport in which only men could take part. If a woman wanted to run a section or even the whole route, she had to do so without wearing an entry number, in other words, without officially taking part in the competition – women didn't count. Switzer, however, wanted to compete and wanted a number to show it.

During the race, one of the managers, Jock Semple, tried to stop her. He even yelled: "Get out of my race and give me back the number!"

But he could not reach her because her boyfriend and other runners created a kind of barrier to make sure that Switzer could carry on. During the race, Switzer was photographed as a great curiosity, chased to stop her from continuing, and finally disqualified once she had crossed the finish line, but this did not discourage her. On the contrary.

The Boston Marathon was only the beginning of Switzer's career as a true professional runner. She won the New York marathon in 1974 and came second in the Boston Marathon of 1975, achieving her best-ever time: two hours, 51 minutes and 37 seconds.

Switzer knew – and demonstrated – that running was for everyone, and that is why for more than 40 years she was one of the most important activists in women's sport. Thanks to her successes and her struggle, after many years and much effort, women are able to compete in a marathon.

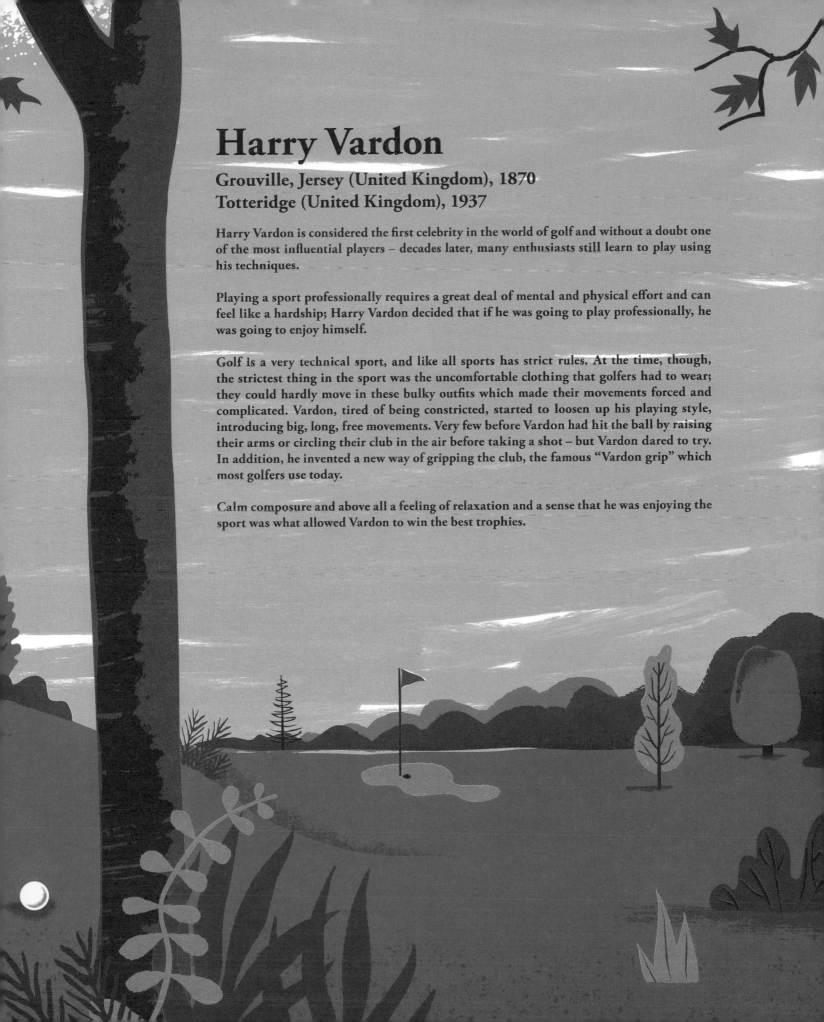

Harry Vardon

Grouville, Jersey (United Kingdom), 1870
Totteridge (United Kingdom), 1937

Harry Vardon is considered the first celebrity in the world of golf and without a doubt one of the most influential players – decades later, many enthusiasts still learn to play using his techniques.

Playing a sport professionally requires a great deal of mental and physical effort and can feel like a hardship; Harry Vardon decided that if he was going to play professionally, he was going to enjoy himself.

Golf is a very technical sport, and like all sports has strict rules. At the time, though, the strictest thing in the sport was the uncomfortable clothing that golfers had to wear; they could hardly move in these bulky outfits which made their movements forced and complicated. Vardon, tired of being constricted, started to loosen up his playing style, introducing big, long, free movements. Very few before Vardon had hit the ball by raising their arms or circling their club in the air before taking a shot – but Vardon dared to try. In addition, he invented a new way of gripping the club, the famous "Vardon grip" which most golfers use today.

Calm composure and above all a feeling of relaxation and a sense that he was enjoying the sport was what allowed Vardon to win the best trophies.

Chester Williams

Western Cape (South Africa), 1970 – Cape Town (South Africa), 2019

Chester Wiliams was the only black player on the South African rugby team which won the Rugby World Cup in 1995. Many think that this was Williams' greatest achievement, although that was not the case. A much more important and significant role was reserved for him, one that would mark a historic change. He was the first black rugby player chosen to play in a final and, in the turbulent world of the time, became a symbol for the end of apartheid in South Africa.

Williams and Nelson Mandela, South Africa's president, met before the cup took place to discuss how the games could bring the country together after apartheid. The abiding image of that legendary tournament is not the scoreboard, the points, the brilliant moves, or even the players, it is Nelson Mandela, dressed in the Springboks cap and shirt, presenting the cup.

It had taken a lot to get to that point. The world was changing and for the first time these small improvements were happening even in the world of sport, in front of hundreds of thousands of spectators.

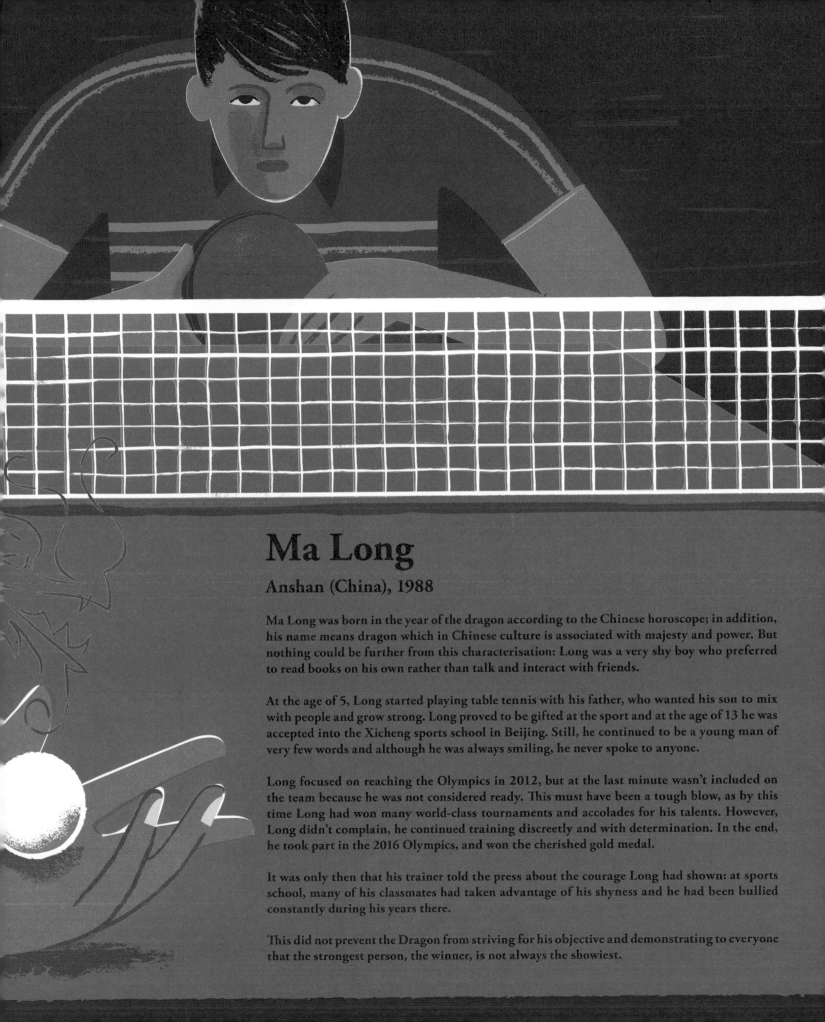

Ma Long
Anshan (China), 1988

Ma Long was born in the year of the dragon according to the Chinese horoscope; in addition, his name means dragon which in Chinese culture is associated with majesty and power. But nothing could be further from this characterisation: Long was a very shy boy who preferred to read books on his own rather than talk and interact with friends.

At the age of 5, Long started playing table tennis with his father, who wanted his son to mix with people and grow strong. Long proved to be gifted at the sport and at the age of 13 he was accepted into the Xicheng sports school in Beijing. Still, he continued to be a young man of very few words and although he was always smiling, he never spoke to anyone.

Long focused on reaching the Olympics in 2012, but at the last minute wasn't included on the team because he was not considered ready. This must have been a tough blow, as by this time Long had won many world-class tournaments and accolades for his talents. However, Long didn't complain, he continued training discreetly and with determination. In the end, he took part in the 2016 Olympics, and won the cherished gold medal.

It was only then that his trainer told the press about the courage Long had shown: at sports school, many of his classmates had taken advantage of his shyness and he had been bullied constantly during his years there.

This did not prevent the Dragon from striving for his objective and demonstrating to everyone that the strongest person, the winner, is not always the showiest.

Patti McGee

Santa Monica, California (USA), 1945

Patti McGee, like her friends, spent every free moment of her childhood on the beach, waiting for the sea to offer up the best surfing waves. But the waves were unreliable and McGee and her friends were soon looking for a way to experience the same sensations that surfing gave them, but on asphalt. Having fun was everything, and soon skateboarding became her passion.

McGee's first wooden skateboard was a gift from her brother: he had made it himself in a carpenter's shop in the neighbourhood where they lived. She spent hours and hours on this first board, barefoot most of the time as if she were still on the sea. McGee easily mastered the board and before long she became USA national skateboarding champion and also the fastest girl on a skateboard, reaching 46 miles per hour.

She appeared on the covers of some of the most important magazines in the world, including Life, which photographed her doing her legendary "handstand".

McGee ignored those people who said that this sport was not for girls or that girls were not built to be constantly falling down. McGee's powerful victory was to demonstrate to the world that sports are for everyone.